Cooking With Chia

By Gloria Hoover

Cooking with Chia. Copyright 2007 by Gloria Hoover. All rights reserved. No part of this book may be used or reproduced in any manner whatsoever without the written permission of the author except in the case of brief quotations embodied in critical articles and reviews. For information about obtaining reproduction rights, please contact the author.

This book is intended as an educational and informational resource. The publisher and author expressly disclaim any responsibility or liability in connection with the use of this book.

ISBN: 978-1-4303-2434-8

Table of Contents

Chia Food of the Aztecs	5
Chia Basics	9
Breakfast	11
For Lunch or Dinner	23
Salad Dressings	55
Smoothies/Drinks	71
Desserts & Other Good Stuff	87

Chia - Food of the Aztecs

Chia seeds are one of the most nutritious foods of nature. Since Chia has a long history of hundreds of years of being used as a human and animal energy food source the United States Dept of Agriculture lists Chia as food product.

Much has been written about the history of Chia and how it was a staple food of the Native Peoples of the Americas from the time of the Aztecs until the current time period.

As more people are discovering the energy, the health benefits, nutrition and even the weight loss benefits they are asking "How can I use chia in my daily diet?" "What are the nutrition benefits of chia"?

Chia has several unique properties that include:

- Can absorb at least 9 times its weight in liquid forming a gel
- Can be toasted to use (this will stop the gelling process) yet toasting does not change the nutrition
- Does not need to be ground for use in baking, cooking or breading of other foods
- Is gluten free, low in sodium, low in saturated fat, low in carbohydrates
- If stored in a dry, cool place has an extended shelf life
- Has no known allergenic reactions
- Children like the taste
- Can be sprouted and the sprouts used in salads or sandwiches
- Chia gel is easy to make and can be added to other food products

Chia is easy to digest, easy to add to any one's diet. So let's explore Chia.

WHICH IS BETTER??

Should I use chia seeds, sprouts, gel, ground or whole, and what about chia oil?

Chia seeds, gel, and oil all have the same nutrition except that the oil does not contain the fiber. Chia seeds and gel can be used "as is" or in baking, cooking or toasted. Chia oil can NOT be used from cooking as the heat will oxide the compounds found in the oil. The chia seed outer hull forms a barrier to prevent the oxidation when using the whole seeds in cooking or baking. Sprouts have the same nutrition but like the oil lack the fiber of the seeds.

Remember chia seeds do not need to be ground to be used in any method of cooking or baking. This makes them very easy to add to your diet.

But what about the flavor? Chia has almost no flavor. Most people can't taste the slight nutty taste that it has, and when blended with other foods even that taste is absorbed. When Chia is toasted the nutty flavor is just a little more pronounced and the gelling properties disappear.

It really is more of a personal preference than a nutritional difference of which chia product you use.

WHAT ARE THE BENEFITS OF CHIA?

Chia seeds are high in omega-3 and fiber. Additionally they contain the highest percentage of alpha-linolenic acid and linolenic acid percentages of any crop. Alpha-linolenic acid has been shown to possibly help to prevent cancer and to protect against other diseases. More research is being done at this time.

Chia seeds contain a higher protein percent than wheat, corn, rice or oats. Yet chia is gluten free. Chia is also high in amino acids that include Aspartic acid, Threonine, Serine, Valine, Lysine, Proline as well as others. When chia is mixed with other grains it can produce a complete protein source. This is helpful for all people especially vegans or people with digestive or diet restrictions.

Chia is a good source of B vitamins. Research shows that low levels of B vitamins are linked to an increase risk of heart disease and stroke. Chia is higher in niacin than corn, soybeans, and rice.

Chia is also an excellent source of calcium, phosphorus, magnesium, potassium, iron, zinc and copper. Chia contains more calcium, phosphorus, potassium then wheat, rice, barley, oats and corn. Chia also contains 6 times more calcium, 11 times more phosphorus and 4 times more potassium than milk.

Chia seed is a source of dietary fiber as well as the ability to slow the absorption of carbohydrates and glucose levels for several hours. This has several benefits from feeling fuller longer to the lower glucose levels and spikes that can occur.

With the high levels of calcium, chia may help in fighting off Osteoporosis and other bone lose diseases.

Reports have also shown that chia may be helpful in Crohn's disease, inflammatory bowl disease, ulcerative colitis. More research is needed to determine how this occurs.

As mentioned Chia is low in sodium, little flavor, easy to use but packs a lot of nutrition in a small package.

Chia is considered to be food by the USDA with a long history of safe usage. The Aztecs used Chia as one of their food staples for the health, physical endurance and even in important celebrations. During the time of the Spanish invasion, the growing of chia was halted and only small family farms remained until recently. Today, chia can become a stable in your diet with just a little thought as to how to incorporate this marvelous little seed.

It can be as easy as sprinkling chia seeds on your favorite breakfast cereal or adding a tablespoon of chia to your bowl of soup. It is easy to add chia to any of your favorite recipes, food or prepared meals. An example of easy - sprinkle it on your slice of pizza! How's that of easy?

The following recipes are a combination of old favorites and new updated cuisine showing just how easy adding chia to your diet is.

CHIA BASICS

Toasting Chia Seeds

Heat a small skillet over high heat. Add chia seeds and toast for 2 minutes. Cool, store in an air tight container, use as desired. Shelf life is at least two years.

Chia Gel

Place nine parts of water to one part of chia - example 8 ounces of water to one ounce of chia seeds - into a seal able plastic or glass container. Mix with a fork or wire whisk. Wait a few minutes then stir again to break up any clumps. Let stand about 10 minutes, stir again. The chia gel is ready to use. Store up to two weeks in the refrigerator.

Quick & Easy Ways to Use Chia Seeds

For fewer calories and fat just mix ½ cup chia gel with

½ cup store brought salad dressing
½ cup ketchup
½ cup soft butter
½ cup peanut butter or other nut butter
½ cup Nutella
½ cup tomato sauce
½ cup whipped topping
½ cup ice cream topping sauce
½ cup pancake syrup
Or any other type of liquid product

Not only are there fewer calories and fat grams you have increased the fiber, omega-3, protein, calcium, B vitamins.

Sprinkle chia seeds on

Salads
Ice cream
Yogurt
Sandwiches
Cooked vegetables
Fresh fruit
Soups
Toasted buttered breads and rolls

BREAKFAST

Chia Bran Muffins
Makes 15 muffins

Ingredients

1 ½ cups all-purpose flour
¾ cup chia seed
¾ cup oat bran
1 cup packed brown sugar
2 tablespoons cooking oil
2 teaspoons baking soda
2 cups shredded carrots
1 teaspoon baking powder
2 apples, peeled and shredded
1 teaspoon salt
½ cup raisins
2 teaspoons ground cinnamon

¾ cup skim milk
2 eggs, beaten
1 teaspoon vanilla

Directions

Heat the oven to 350 degrees. Grease or lightly spray the muffin tins with cooking oil or use the paper liners.

In a small bowl, mix the milk, beaten eggs, vanilla, oil and chia seeds. Let set about 5 minutes.

In a large bowl, mix together the flour, oat bran, brown sugar, baking soda, baking powder, salt and cinnamon. Add the milk mixture and mix until just blended. Stir in the apples, raisins and carrots. Fill the prepare muffin cups 2/3 full of batter.

Bake for 15 to 20 minutes or until a toothpick comes out clean.

Chia Blueberry Pancakes
Makes 4 pancakes (recipe can be doubled)

Ingredients

1 ½ cups of a dry pancake mix (any type of your choice we use Bisquick)
½ cup chia seeds
1 cup skim milk or soy, rice, nut milk
2 eggs or egg substitute
1 cup fresh or frozen blueberries

Directions

Mix the chia seeds with the milk of choice and let set about 5 minutes. In a medium size mixing bowl add the pancake mix. In a separate bowl or large measuring cup whisk the eggs or egg substitute with the chia milk mixture. Pour the liquid into the bowl with the pancake mix and stir until just moistened or combined.

While mixing set a nonstick skillet or griddle over medium heat, spray with a light coating of vegetable oil.

When the skillet/griddle is hot, spoon ¼ cupfuls of batter onto the skillet. Sprinkle with as many blueberries as desired. Cook until bubbles form on the surface, flip and cook until browned on the other side.

Gluten Free Hot Chia Cereal

Makes 4 servings

Ingredients

½ cup Buckwheat Kernels which can be called Roasted Kasha
¼ cup chia seeds
½ teaspoon salt
½ teaspoon butter
3 cups of milk or 2 ½ cups water

Directions

In a heavy saucepan bring milk (or water is using) to a boil. Slowly stir in the buckwheat kernels and the chia seed, then add the butter and salt. Boil 10 to 12 minutes stirring occasionally.

Serve hot with milk / soy / cream and honey to sweeten.

Note: Buckwheat is high in potassium, phosphorus and contains 50% more Vitamin B than wheat. Buckwheat is also high in protein.

Breakfast Pizza
12 Slices

Ingredients
Flour for dusting
2 Tablespoons of Extra Virgin Olive oil
½ large Red onion, diced
7 Medium mushrooms, sliced
1 Green pepper, seeded, diced
3 Garlic cloves minced
1 Tablespoon each chopped Basil and Parsley leaves
½ cup cooked ham, diced
2 Cooked bacon slices, chopped
2 Cooked sausage links, sliced
Salt and pepper to taste
½ cup Tomato sauce
5 eggs beaten
1 cup Shredded Mozzarella cheese
¼ cup Parmesan cheese, shredded

Directions

Preheat oven to 375 degrees.

Fit dough into a 12-in. tart pan with removable bottom or pizza pan.

Heat medium skillet over high heat. Add oil, onion, mushrooms,
green peppers, garlic, basil and parsley; sauté until onions are tender.
Reduce heat to medium; add ham, bacon and sausage. Cook 1 minute. Season
with salt and pepper. Remove from heat.

Spread crust with tomato sauce. Ladle vegetable/meat mixture over crust,
spreading evenly. Pour beaten eggs on top. Sprinkle with cheeses. Bake 12
minutes or until cheese is golden brown.

Release pizza from pan. Cut into wedges. Serve immediately.

Chia Breakfast Strata
Serves 6

Ingredients

4 slices of white bread, cut into ½ dice
1 ½ sliced peaches or other fruit of your choice
6 ounces soft cheese grated
1 - 12 ounce can evaporated milk
4 eggs lightly beaten or 1 cup of egg substitute
2 Tablespoons of sugar or other sweetener
2 teaspoons ground cinnamon
1 teaspoons vanilla extract
¼ cup of chia seeds

Directions

The day before baking - Soak the chia seeds in the evaporated milk for at least 5 minutes. In a large mixing bowl combine the milk and chia mixture with the eggs, sugar, cinnamon and vanilla and mix well. Arrange half of the bread in the bottom of a 8 by 11 inch baking dish. Lay half of the peaches or other fruit over the bread, layer half of the cheese over the fruit. Repeat the layers.

Pour the liquid mixture over the bread layers, cover with plastic wrap and refrigerate overnight.

The next day remove the dish from the refrigerator 1 hour before baking. Then place in a cold oven. Turn the oven on at 350 degrees and bake 1 hour and 15 minutes or until the liquid is absorbed and the top is just a light brown. Serve warm.

Cinnamon Granola
Makes 7 cups

Ingredients:
4 cups old-fashioned oats
1 1/2 cup sliced almonds
1/2 cup packed light brown sugar
1/2 teaspoon salt
1/2 teaspoon ground cinnamon
1/4 cup vegetable oil
1/4 cup honey
1 teaspoon vanilla extract
1 1/2 cup raisins
½ cup chia seeds

Directions:

Preheat oven to 300 F. In a bowl combine the chia, oats, almonds, brown sugar, salt and cinnamon. In a saucepan over medium heat warm the oil and honey. Whisk in vanilla.

Carefully pour the liquid over the oat mixture. Stir gently with a wooden spoon; finish mixing by hand. Spread granola in a 15x10 inch baking pan sprayed or coated with cooking oil.

Bake 40 minutes, stirring every 15 minutes. Transfer granola pan to a rack to cool completely. Stir in raisins. When cool place the granola in an airtight container or self-sealing plastic bag. Store at room temperature for 1 week or in the freezer for 3 months.

Blueberry Whole Wheat Pancakes
Makes 24 4 inch pancakes

Ingredients
2 cups all-purpose flour
1 cup whole wheat flour
½ cups buttermilk
1 ½ teaspoons baking soda
2 large eggs
1 teaspoon salt
1 Tablespoon sugar
¼ cup chia seed
2 cups blueberries
1 ½ Tablespoons melted butter

Directions

In a bowl whisk together the buttermilk, eggs and gradually add the flours, baking soda, sugar and chia seeds. Whisk the batter until just combined and smooth. Heat a griddle over medium high heat until it is hot enough to make drops of water "bounce". Brush with the melted butter. Working in batches, pour the batter onto to griddle by ½ cup measuring cup or ladle, top pancakes with the blueberries. Cook about 2 minutes per side or until they are golden brown. Can be keep warm in a preheated 200 degree oven until ready to serve.

Chile Relleno Omelet
Serves 2

Ingredients

1 can green chilies either whole or diced if whole diced them
½ cup grated Monterey Jack Cheese or your favorite
5 eggs lightly beaten
4 Tablespoons chia seed
1 Tablespoon butter

Salsa to serve

Directions

Melt ½ tablespoon of butter in a nonstick omelet pan over medium heat. When hot pour in half of the eggs. Using a spatula to lift up the omelet's edges to allow any remaining liquid egg to flow underneath. Keep the skillet moving until the eggs are set. Add ½ of the grated cheese and 2 tablespoons of chia seed. Fold the omelet over and slide onto a plate. Repeat with the other half of the ingredients.

Green Chili Frittata
Serves 2

Ingredients

1 Tablespoon olive oil
½ cup chopped onion
½ cup chopped red bell pepper
½ cup canned diced green chili peppers
2 eggs lightly beaten or egg substitute
1 teaspoons ground red chili pepper
¾ cup shredded Cheddar cheese
4 Tablespoons chia seed

Directions

Over medium heat, heat the olive oil in a large skillet. Sauté the onion and bell pepper until softened about 7 minutes. Add the green diced chili pepper and the chia seeds. Pour the egg over the top of the mixture in the skillet. Cook on low heat until almost set. Sprinkle the top with the cheddar cheese cover for 1 minute. Remove from the skillet to a serving platter and cut into wedges.

LUNCH OR DINNER

Chia Cheese Enchiladas
Serves 4

Ingredients

8 ounces shredded cheese (Mexican blend or cheddar are nice choices)
6 green onions chopped into ¼ pieces - green and white parts
2 teaspoons ground cumin
8 ounces of cream cheese at room temperature
8 enchilada size tortillas (corn or flour)
1 10 ounce can Enchilada Sauce
8 Tablespoons chia seeds

Directions

Preheat oven to 400 degrees. Spray a 9 x 13 inch baking dish with vegetable spray. Reserve about 4 ounces of the shredded cheese for the topping.

In a medium bowl, combine the remaining cheese, onions, cumin, chia seeds. Spread the softening cream cheese equality on the tortilla, top with the onion/chia mixture. Roll the tortillas and place seam side down in the baking dish. Pour the enchilada sauce over the top of tortillas, sprinkle the remaining cheese over the top of the sauce. Bake about 15 to 20 minutes until golden brown and bubbly.

Baked Tuna Sandwiches
Makes 6 large sandwiches

Ingredients

1 package hamburger buns
1 can tuna drained (can be made with canned chicken)
2 Tablespoons minced onions
2 Tablespoons minced olives
½ cup Shredded cheese of your choice (cheddar is nice)
2 Tablespoons chopped green pepper
4 Tablespoons chia seed
Mayonnaise to moisten

Directions

Preheat oven to 350 degrees

In a large mixing bowl, combine all ingredients except hamburger buns. When the ingredients are mixed, place equal amounts of the mixture on the hamburger buns. Wrap the buns in aluminum foil and bake for 20 minutes. Serve hot. If any leftovers just reheat them the next day.

Chia Coated Fish

Ingredients

Fish fillets of your choice - we suggest Tilapia, cod, bass
    or similar type
Chia seeds
Spices of your choice - examples are Old Bay, Mexican, Grilling Fish Rubs

Heat a skillet with just enough cooking oil to coat the bottom of the pan, more if desired.

While the skillet is heating, mix the seasonings and chia seeds in a flat dish. Then dredge the fish in the mixture until coated on both sides. Place the fish in the skillet and cook about 5 to 7 minutes then turn and continue cooking until fish flakes and is done.

The chia seeds will add a slightly nutty flavor to the fish.

Serve with your favorite sauce.

Chia Coated Tofu

Ingredients

Slices of your favorite tofu lightly sprayed with cooking oil
Chia seeds
Spices of your choice - examples are Old Bay, Mexican, Grilling Fish Rubs

Heat a skillet with just enough cooking oil to coat the bottom of the pan, more if desired.

While the skillet is heating, mix the seasonings and chia seeds in a flat dish. Then dredge the tofu in the mixture until coated on both sides. Place the tofu in the skillet and cook about 5 to 7 minutes then turn and continue cooking until done.

The chia seeds will add a slightly nutty flavor and a crunch to the tofu.

Serve with your favorite sauce.

Chia Hamburgers

1 pound or so of good hamburger
¼ cup of chia seeds

Mix the chia seeds with the hamburger, form into patties and broil or grill until done (instant read thermometer says 165 degrees). Serve on a bun with your favorite "fixings"

A real quick way to add to hamburgers or other sandwiches is to sprinkle a tablespoon of chia seeds on the bun/bread just prior to serving.

Curry Onions
Makes 6 servings

Ingredients

12 medium onions sliced ¼ inch thick
Cooking oil, butter or margarine
1 teaspoon curry powder (We suggest Madras)
2 teaspoons lemon juice
1 tablespoon chia seeds
Salt and pepper to taste
Optional soy sauce

Directions

Heat the cooking oil, butter or margarine in a large skillet. Sauté the onions slowly, turning often for about 25 to 30 minutes until they are golden.

Stir in the curry powder, lemon juice, chia seeds, salt and pepper and soy sauce if using.

Toss lightly and serve as a side to meat, pork or use as a hamburger topping.

Chia Mashed Sweet Potatoes
Serves 4

Ingredients

3 pounds of sweet potatoes (about 4 medium)
¼ cup of chia seeds
Butter to taste
Milk either cow's, soy, rice or nut

Directions

Either microwave cook the sweet potatoes just as would baked potatoes or peel, slice and boil until tender.

Mash sweet potatoes with a potato masher until smooth, add the butter and chia seeds. Stir in enough milk to make the mixture smooth. Add salt and pepper to taste.

Chia Quinoa Salad
Makes app. 6 servings

Ingredients:

2 Cups cooked and cooled Quinoa
    See side of box for cooking instructions
1 Cup chopped parsley
½ cup chopped green onions
medium Garlic clove either minced or pressed
1 Tablespoon finely chopped fresh Basil or ½ teaspoon
    dried
½ cup Lemon Juice
¼ cup Olive Oil Extra Virgin preferred
¼ cup chia seeds
Salt and pepper to taste

Directions:

Place all ingredients into a large bowl, mix together until all ingredients are lightly coated with the olive oil. Cover and place in the refrigerator to chill for at least 1 hour or more to allow the flavors to blend.

Celery au Gratin
Serves 4 to 6

2 small bunches celery
1/3 pound grated Cheddar cheese
1/3 cup milk (cow's, rice, soy or nut)
1 cup soft day-old bread crumbs mixed with 3 tablespoons
    chia seed
1 tablespoon melted butter or margarine

Directions

Wash and clean celery, removing the top leaves and bottom portions. Cut stalks lengthwise into quarters. If the stalks are really long, cut into halves crosswise),

In a covered oven safe skillet, place the celery and enough salted water to cover. Simmer gently until just tender, about 20 minutes but do not overcook. When tender drain.

In a other saucepan or microwave, melt the cheese in the milk stirring until smooth.

Pour the cheese mixture over the celery, sprinkle with the chia bread crumbs that were tossed with the melted butter.

If the skillet handle is not of metal or oven safe, wrap in aluminum foil. Place the skillet under the broiler till the mixture is bubbly and brown about 7 to 9 minutes.

Skillet Squash
Serves 4

Ingredients

2 Tablespoons butter, margarine or cooking oil
4 cups thinly sliced zucchini or other summer squash
1 thinly sliced small onion
Salt and pepper to taste
¼ cup water or 2 tomatoes peeled and sliced thin
½ cup grated Cheddar cheese
¼ cup chia seeds

Directions

Melt butter, margarine or cooking oil in a large skillet. Add the squash, onion, salt, pepper and either the water or the tomatoes. Simmer covered about 15 minutes or until soft.

While that is cooking, mix the Cheddar cheese and chia seed until combined.

When the zucchini is cooked, move to a serving dish. Then sprinkle the chia/cheese mixture over the top, let melt and then serve hot.

Cheeseburger Pie
Serves 6

Ingredients

1 pound ground hamburger or turkey
1 large onion chopped
1 cup shredded Cheddar cheese
1 cup of milk (cow's, rice, soy or nut)
½ cup baking mix such as Bisquick
2 eggs beaten
¼ cup chia seeds
Salt and pepper to taste

Directions

Preheat oven to 400 degrees. Spray or grease a 9 inch baking dish.

Brown the ground meat and onion. In a mixing bowl, add the eggs, baking mix, milk and cheese. Spread the ground meat and onion in the baking dish, sprinkle with the chia seeds. Pour the liquid mixture over the top.

Bake about 30 minutes or until a toothpick inserted in the center comes out clean.

Watermelon Salad With Tomato and Chia
Serves 8

Ingredients

½ large watermelon preferably seedless cut into ¼ inch slices with rind removed.
1 pint baby grape tomatoes cut in quarters
½ cup chia seeds
½ cup fresh basil cut into fine strips
1 cup fresh mint leaves cut into fine strips
Chia Oil
Balsamic vinegar
Salt and pepper to taste

Directions

Arrange the watermelon pieces on a serving platter. Place the tomato amongst the watermelon and sprinkle with the basil, mint and chia seeds. Drizzle with the chia oil and vinegar. Add a little salt and pepper. Serve at room temperature.

Salmon Cakes
Serves 4

Ingredients
2 cans of canned Salmon or 1 pound poached fresh
    Salmon
¼ cup cracker crumbs
2 eggs beaten
1 ½ teaspoons Old Bay Seasoning or other seasoning of
    your choice
¼ cup chia seeds

Mix all the ingredients together in a bowl. If the mixture is a little dry add a little olive oil to moisten. Form the mixture into equal patties (will make app. 8 patties).

To Bake - Preheat oven to 350 degrees. Spray or coat the bottom of a baking dish with cooking oil. Place the salmon patties in the pan and back about 20 minutes or until golden brown.

To pan fry/sauté - in a large skillet add enough cooking oil to coat the bottom of the pan. On medium high heat, fry the patties about 8 minutes per side.

Meat Loaf
Serves 4 to 6

Ingredients

1 pound ground beef or turkey
2 cups warm milk
½ cup bread crumbs
¼ cup chia seeds
1 small onion chopped
Salt and pepper to taste
¼ cup catsup
2 slight beaten eggs

Directions

Preheat oven to 350 degrees.

In a large mixing bowl combine all the ingredients and mix thoroughly. Put the mixture into a loaf pan or other baking dish. Bake 1 hour to 1 hour 20 minutes or until done.

Chili Beans
Serves 4 to 6

Ingredients

2 pounds ground beef or turkey
1 medium onion chopped
2 cans kidney beans drained
1 teaspoons salt
1 can diced tomatoes
1 Tablespoon chili pepper seasoning (Gerhart's is suggested)
2 Tablespoons sugar
1 Tablespoon chia seed per serving

Directions

Brown the ground meat and onion in a large skillet over medium high heat. When brown add the kidney beans, salt, tomatoes, chili pepper seasoning and simmer over low heat for about 1 hour. Add the sugar (this blends all the flavors and smooth the acid of the tomatoes). When serving add the chia seed to each bowl.

Sloppy Joes
Serves 4

Ingredients

1 pound ground beef or turkey
1 small onion chopped
1 8 ounce can tomato sauce
¼ cup catsup
¼ cup water
Salt and pepper to taste
1 Tablespoon chia seed per serving

Directions

In a skillet over medium heat brown the ground meat and onion. When browned, salt and pepper to taste, adding the tomato sauce, catsup and water. Simmer for 15 to 20 minutes. To serve divide among 4 sandwich buns, topping with the chia seed.

Huntington Chicken
Serves 6

Ingredients

4 pound chicken cooked, boned and cut into bite sized pieces
½ cup uncooked macaroni - cooked in boiling salt water until tender
½ Pound Cheddar cheese cubed into ½ inch pieces
2 cups dry bread crumbs
¼ cup chia seeds
½ cup heavy cream

Make a thin sauce of
4 cups of chicken broth
8 Tablespoons of flour

Directions

Preheat oven to 325 degrees.

Brown the bread crumbs and chia in ½ stick of butter over medium heat. Stir in cream. Set aside. In a large mixing bowl stir together all ingredients except the bread crumb mixture. Pour the mixing bowl ingredients into a 9 by 13 inch baking dish. Top with the bread crumb mixture. Bake for 45 minutes. Serve hot

Old Fashion Tuna Casserole
Serves 4 to 6

Ingredients
1 Tbsp butter or olive oil
1/2 cup diced onion
1/2 cup diced celery
1 can cream of mushroom soup
1/2 cup water or milk
8 ounce frozen peas
1 (6-ounce) can tuna packed in water or oil drained
1 cup buttered bread crumbs or crushed plain potato chips
8 ounces packaged wide noodles, cooked al dente
¼ cup chia seeds

Directions:
Preheat oven to 400 degrees F. Spray a casserole dish with vegetable oil or lightly grease.

In a large saucepan, sauté onion and celery in the butter or olive oil until they are barely soft, but not mushy.

Add mushroom soup, water, and peas. Bring to a simmer, stirring to dissolve soup and mix in the chia seed. When it begins to boil, turn off heat and gently fold in tuna..

Add cooked noodles and toss to coat with sauce. Pour into prepared casserole and top with bread crumbs or potato chips. Bake 30 to 40 minutes until heated through and topping is lightly browned.

Mediterranean Chicken
Serves 4

Ingredients
4 skinless boneless chicken breasts
1 can chicken broth or stock
4 teaspoons capers
¼ cup green olives roughly chopped
½ cup all-purpose flour
3 gloves of garlic roughly chopped
1/3 cup chia seed
Salt and pepper to taste

Vegetable oil for sautéing
Directions

One at time place the chicken breast between layers of plastic wrap, with the smooth side of a meat mallet or with a rolling pin pound each breast until it is an even thinnest about ¼ inch thick.

In a large skillet, heat over medium heat about ¼ inch of vegetable oil.

In a flat dish, place the flour, salt and pepper. Dredge each chicken breast in the flour coating on both sides.

When the skillet is hot, place the chicken into the oil, being careful not to splatter. Cook until just brown on each side.

Stir in the chicken broth, capers, olives, garlic and chia seeds. Turn the heat down to a simmer. Simmer for 30 minutes. Serve with noodles or polenta.

Creamy Carrot Casserole
Serves 8

Ingredients

5 cups of sliced, peeled carrots
1 cup mayonnaise type salad dressing
½ cup onion finely chopped
1 tablespoon prepared horseradish
Salt and pepper to taste
¼ cup chia seeds
1 Tablespoon butter or margarine or other oil

Directions

At least 4 hours to 24 hours ahead of time - cook carrots in boiling water until tender, drain. Pour into a 2 quart baking dish. In a small mixing bowl, combine the salad dressing, onion, horseradish, salt and pepper, stir until smooth. Mix into the dish with the carrots. Cover and refrigerate for 4 to 24 hours.

Preheat the oven to 350 degrees. Remove the baking dish from the refrigerator and uncover. Melt butter in a sauce pan or microwave, stir in the chia seeds and sprinkle over the carrots. Bake for 20 minutes or until heated.

Bean Soup
Serves 8

Ingredients

1 pound of white beans or pinto beans
Water to soak the beans
4 cups of vegetable stock
½ cup chia seeds
1 Bay leaf
1 Teaspoons of each oregano, marjoram, thyme, salt and pepper
If desired a dash or two of hot pepper sauce and a pinch of dried pepper flakes

Directions

Soak the beans overnight with enough water for them to expand. When ready to cook, place the beans, stock and seasonings in a large stock pot. Simmer over low heat for 1 to 1 hr and 30 minutes or until tender. Remove from the heat and stir in the chia seeds. The chia will help to thicken the soup.

When ready to cook, drain the beans and discard the water. In a stock add all the ingredients, bring to a boil, then reduce the heat to simmer for about 1 hour or until the beans are tender.

Bean Soup II
Serves 4

Ingredients

1 Tablespoon Extra Virgin Olive Oil
1 medium onion chopped
1 large carrot peeled and finely chopped
1 celery stalk, finely chopped
4 cloves garlic chopped
3 cups Organic vegetable broth
¼ cup chia seeds
1 15 ounce can of either Navy or Great Northern white beans, drained and washed
Salt and pepper to taste

Directions

In a bowl or measuring cup mix the chia seeds and vegetable broth, stirring to remove lumps.

In a large stock pot, over medium heat add the olive oil. When hot, add the onion, carrot, celery and cooking about 10 minutes. Add the garlic, cook about 2 minutes. Add the beans and the chia broth and cook for about 15 minutes. Do not boil just simmer the mixture. Ladle into serving bowls.

Greek Baked Eggplant with Chia
Serves 6

Ingredients

2 Tablespoons butter, margarine or cooking oil
1 large onion, diced
1 pound ground beef or turkey
½ pound ground pork or turkey
1 clove garlic minced
1 cup canned tomato sauce
½ cup cold water
¼ teaspoon ground nutmeg
Cooking oil to fry egg plant - start with about 1/8 cup
1 cup flour seasoned with salt and pepper to taste
2 medium eggplants, peeled, sliced lengthwise into ½ inch slices
½ cup grated Parmesan cheese
¼ cup chia seeds

Directions

Heat oven to 350 degrees.

In a large skillet over medium heat melt the 2 tablespoons of butter or cooking oil. When hot add the onion with a pinch of salt and pepper. Sauté for 5 minutes. Add the ground meats and cook about 10 more minutes until the meat is browned. Add the tomato sauce, cold water and nutmeg, simmer for 15 minutes.

In a large skillet, heat the cooking oil to fry the egg plant. Mix the flour with salt and pepper and use to coat the eggplant slices. Fry the eggplant in the oil until light brown. You will need to do several batches.

As you remove the eggplant from the skillet, place about half the slices in the bottom of an 9x13x2 inch baking dish that has been sprayed with cooking oil. Spread half of the meat mixture over the eggplant, then sprinkle that layer with half of the chia seed. Repeat the layers and sprinkle top with Parmesan cheese.

Bake 30 minutes. Serve hot, cut into squares. Nice with crusty bread and a green leafy salad.

PB&J Sandwich
Serves 1

Ingredients

2 Slices of bread (your choice)
Peanut butter - your favorite kind
Jelly - your favorite kind
1 Tablespoon chia seed - more or less if you desire

Directions

Lay the two slices of bread on a plate or cutting board. Put as much peanut butter as you desired on one slice, as much jelly on the other slice, sprinkle the chia on one side. Put the two slices together. Cut if desired, remove the crust if desired. Enjoy.

Lentil Stew
Makes 4 servings

Ingredients

9 ounces rinsed uncooked lentils
1 quart water
12 ounces white or gold potatoes, peeled and diced into ½ inch cubes
1 cup each carrot, onion, celery diced
2 garlic cloves minced
1 bay leaf
½ teaspoon ground cumin
½ teaspoon each of dried thyme, dried oregano, black pepper
¼ cup chia seed
Salt to taste

Directions

In a medium size stock pot combine the lentils and water; bring to a boil. Reduce the heat to low, cover and simmer until lentils are tender, about 25 minutes.

Add the remaining ingredients to the lentils, stir to combine; cover and continue cooking on low heat until the potatoes are tender, about 20 minutes. Remove the bay leaf and serve.

Southwestern Chicken
Serves 1

Ingredients

1 boneless skinless chicken breast
2 Tablespoons of flour
1 teaspoon of chia seed
1 teaspoon butter
3 Tablespoons pico de gallo
1 slice of pepper jack cheese
Salt and pepper to taste
Vegetable spray

Directions

Spray a skillet with vegetable spray and over medium high heat melt the butter. While the skillet is heating, mix the flour and chia seed in a small flat dish. Coat the chicken on both sides with the flour/chia mixture.

Sauté the chicken until done about 7 minutes per side. Top with the pico de gallo, top with the cheese slice. Cover the skillet for just a few seconds until the cheese is melted.

Serve on a bun, or with rice.

Sauté Vegetables
Makes 3 cups

Ingredients

1 ½ cups zucchini ribbons
1 ½ cups carrot ribbons
1 Tablespoon chia seeds
2 Tablespoons unsalted butter
1 Tablespoons finely chopped fresh parsley
Salt and pepper to taste

Directions

Cut the zucchini and carrot into ribbons using a vegetable peeler.

In a large skillet over medium heat, melt the butter. Add the ribbons of zucchini and carrots, the chia seeds and salt and pepper. Cover and cook for 5 minutes or until the vegetables are tender.

Remove from the heat, and place in a serving bowl, add the parsley.

Stewed Eggplant
Serves 2

Ingredients

1 small eggplant, peeled, diced into ½ inc cubes
2 cups of diced peeled tomatoes or 1 can tomatoes
1 medium onion, sliced into ¼ inch slices
1 teaspoon oregano
1 teaspoon thyme
1 teaspoon basil
1 Tablespoon chia seed
Salt and pepper to taste
1 Tablespoon vegetable oil (plus more as needed) or broth works well

Directions

In a large skillet over medium heat, add the cooking oil or broth until hot. Add the sliced onions and cook until tender about 15 minutes. Add either cooking oil or broth as needed to moisten the onion, add the egg plant and stir. Add the oregano, thyme, basil, chia seed, tomatoes, salt and pepper. Cover and cook for 15 minutes or until the egg plant is tender.

Chia Corn Chowder
Serves 4

Ingredients

1 Tablespoons Extra Virgin Olive Oil
1 medium onion, cut into dice
2 stalks of celery diced
2 Yukon Gold or Russet Potatoes unpeeled, diced
2 cloves of garlic minced
15 ounces fresh or frozen corn
1 16 ounce can of organic chicken or vegetable broth
3 Cups of milk (your choice of milk)
¼ Cup chia seeds
Salt and pepper to taste.

Directions

In a bowl, mix the chia seeds and milk - sit aside.

In a large stockpot over medium heat add the olive oil. When hot, add the onion and celery; Cook about 7 to 8 minutes. Add the potatoes and cook for about 10 minutes, stirring frequently. Add the garlic and corn cooking for about 2 minutes. Add the broth to the pot, stirring to combine the mixture. Reduce the heat to a simmer and cook uncovered from about 30 minutes. Add the chia/milk mixture, stir and cook until the milk is warm.

Serve hot.

Warm Pea & Potato Salad
Serves 4 (1 cup servings)

Ingredients

1 Pound Yukon gold potatoes, unpeeled cut into 1 inch pieces
½ Cup chopped red or yellow onions
1 Cup peas either fresh or frozen
2 Tablespoons white wine vinegar
2 Teaspoons Dijon style mustard
1/3 cup extra-virgin olive oil or chia oil or a combination of both
2 Tablespoons chopped fresh tarragon
4 Tablespoons chia seeds
Salt and pepper to taste

Cook potatoes in a pot of boiling salt water until tender. Drain well. Return to the pot, the potatoes and onion.

While the potatoes are cooking, cook the peas in a small saucepan with boiling salt water or in the microwave until tender and still bright green. Drain and cool under cold running water.

In a small bowl, whisk the vinegar and mustard until smooth. Whisk in the oil, tarragon, chia seeds, salt and pepper. Toss the warm potatoes and onions with the vinaigrette, stir in the peas. Serve warm or at room temperature.

SALAD DRESSINGS

Egg less Mayonnaise
Makes 1 ½ cups

Ingredients

½ teaspoon salt
½ teaspoon powdered sugar
¼ teaspoon dry mustard
¼ teaspoon paprika
1 Tablespoon vinegar
1 Tablespoon lemon juice
¼ cup chilled evaporated milk
1 cup chilled chia oil

Directions

Whisk the first 8 ingredients until well blended. Add 1/3 cup of the chia oil and beat well. Then add the remaining oil and beat again until creamy and smooth. Serve immediately.

You can do this in a food processor by adding the first 8 ingredients, pulsing until mixed. Drizzle in the chia oil while processing until the mayonnaise is smooth and creamy.

Chia Vinaigrette

2 tablespoons shallot, chopped
1 medium garlic clove, chopped
1 teaspoon coarse-grained mustard
1 tablespoon fresh lemon juice
2 teaspoons balsamic vinegar
1/2 cup chia oil

Make the vinaigrette: In a blender or food processor blend together the shallots, the garlic, the mustard, the lemon juice, the vinegar, and salt and pepper to taste until the mixture is smooth, with the motor running add the oil in a stream, and blend the dressing until it is emulsified.

Orange Yogurt Fruit Salad Dressing
Serves One

Ingredients

1 Small banana
1 Cup low-fat vanilla yogurt
½ cup orange juice
1 Tablespoon Chia seed

Directions
Place the banana, yogurt and orange juice in a blender and process until smooth. Remove from blender, stir in chia seeds and serve over a fruit salad of your choice.

Example is
Pitted cherries, pineapple, orange, honeydew melon with almonds.

Balsamic Vinaigrette
Males 1 2/3 cups

Ingredients

½ Cup Balsamic Vinegar
2 Tablespoons Dijon Mustard
3 small garlic cloves, minced
3 Tablespoons honey
Salt and pepper to taste
½ cup olive oil
½ cup chia oil

Directions

Whisk together all the ingredients except the olive and chia oil. When blended slowly whisk in the olive oil and chia oil. Serve over your favorite salad.

Optional

Instead of using 1 cup total of oil you can mix ½ cup olive oil with ½ cup chia gel (see page 9). This will retain the flavor but with half the fat and calories.

Raspberry Chia Seed Dressing
Makes 2 cups

Ingredients

½ cup sugar
1 teaspoon dry mustard
1 teaspoon salt
1 tablespoon minced onion
1/4 cup raspberry vinegar
½ cup olive oil, vegetable oil or canola oil
½ cup chia oil
2 teaspoons toasted chia seeds (see page 9)

Directions.

In a blender add the raspberry vinegar, onion, mustard, salt, sugar. Pulse for 10 seconds. Then run the blender on low and slowly add the two oils. Pour into a serving container and add the toasted chia seeds.

Option

Instead of using 1 cup total of oil you can mix ½ cup oil with ½ cup chia gel (see page 9). This will retain the flavor but with half the fat and calories.

Chia Seed Salad Dressing
Makes 2 cups

Ingredients

¼ cup honey
¼ cup sugar
¼ cup lemon juice - fresh is best
1 teaspoon dry mustard
1 teaspoon minced onion
¼ teaspoon salt
1 cup olive oil, vegetable oil or oil of you choice
½ cup chia oil
2 Tablespoon toasted chia seeds

Combine the honey, sugar, lemon juice, dry mustard, onion and salt in a blend. Combine until blended. Slowly add the oils until they are emulsified.

Pour into a serving contains and add the toasted chia seeds.

Option

Instead of using 1 cup total of oil you can mix ½ cup oil with ½ cup chia gel (see page 9). This will retain the flavor but with half the fat and calories.

Yogurt Chia Seed Honey Salad Dressing
Makes 1 cup

1 cup plain yogurt
1 tablespoon honey
2 teaspoons orange juice
½ teaspoon cider vinegar
½ teaspoon vanilla extract
2 Tablespoons toasted chia seeds

Directions.

In a mixing bowl whisk all the ingredients together until blended. Place in the refrigerator for at least 30 minutes prior to serving.

Tofu Chia Salad Dressing
Makes 1 cup

Ingredients

¼ cup of water
1 ½ Tablespoons Balsamic vinegar
2 cloves garlic
1 teaspoon Dijon mustard
Salt and pepper to taste
¼ pound firm tofu
1 Tablespoon olive oil
1 Tablespoon chia oil

Directions

Place all the ingredients except the two oils into a blend. Blend until combined. With the blend running slowly add the two oils until the mixture is emulsified.

Option

> Instead of using 2 tablespoons total of oil you can mix 1 tablespoon oil with 1 tablespoon chia gel (see page 9). This will retain the flavor but with half the fat and calories.

Mock Caesar Dressing
Makes 1 cup

Ingredients

1 teaspoons Worcestershire Sauce
3 garlic cloves
¼ cup lemon juice fresh is best
½ cup of olive oil
½ cup of chia oil
½ cup grated Parmesan cheese

Directions

Place all the ingredients in a blender and blend until smooth and emulsified.

Option

Instead of using 1 cup total of oil you can mix ½ cup oil with ½ cup chia gel (see page 9). This will retain the flavor but with half the fat and calories.

Italian Salad Dressing
Makes 1 cup

Ingredients

2 Tablespoons lemon juice fresh is best
3 garlic cloves minced
½ cup of olive oil
½ cup of chia oil
3 Tablespoons dried Italian herbs or if you prefer basil, oregano, parsley
¼ teaspoon crushed dried red pepper for a little heat more if you prefer

Directions.

Place all the ingredients into a mixing bowl and whisk until blended. Can also be placed in a shaker jar and shook until blended.

Option

Instead of using 1 cup total of oil you can mix ½ cup oil with ½ cup chia gel (see page 9). This will retain the flavor but with half the fat and calories.

Cucumber Chia Dressing
Makes 2 2/3 cups

Ingredients
1 Cup Mayonnaise
1 Cup Buttermilk
2 medium cucumbers peeled, seeded and minced
1 Tablespoon minced onion
2 garlic cloves minced or pressed
Salt and pepper to taste
2 Tablespoons chia seeds

Directions

In a small mixing bowl, combine all ingredients until combined and smooth. Refrigerate for several hours prior to serving.

Option

Replace ½ cup of the mayonnaise with ½ cup of chia gel (see page 9) this will reduce the fat and calories.

Quick Easy Chia Salad Dressing

Ingredients

½ cup store brought salad dressing of your choice
½ cup chia gel

Directions

In a small bowl just before serving, combine the two ingredients. This will reduce the fat and calories by half yet the dressing taste the same.

Or you can use the powdered salad dressing mix using ½ of the oil and ½ of chia gel - make according to the package directions.

Roasted Tomato Vinaigrette
Serves 1

Ingredients

2 Roma or plum tomatoes
2 Tablespoons balsamic vinegar
1 Tablespoon chia seed
5 Tablespoons of extra virgin olive oil or chia seed oil or a
 combination of both
Salt and pepper to taste

Directions

Preheat the oven to 400 degrees

Slice the tomatoes in quarters and place on a baking sheet or pan. Sprinkle with the chia seed, salt and pepper. Bake the tomatoes for about 1 hour or until dry. This can be done the day before you plan on using the dressing.

Let the tomatoes cool completely and then finely chop.

In a small mixing bowl, mix the tomato mixture and balsamic vinegar. Slowly add the oil whisk until the mixture is combined. You can also use a salad dressing cruet to mix by shaking until combined.

Lemon Vinaigrette
Makes ¾ cup

Ingredients

1 Tablespoon honey
1 Tablespoon mined onion
2 teaspoon Dijon style mustard
¼ cup fresh lemon juice
¼ cup vegetable oil or chia oil or a combination of both
1 teaspoon chia seed

Directions

> Combine the lemon juice, honey, onions, mustard and chia seeds in a small bowl, whisk to combine. Slowly drizzle in the oil, whisking constantly until emulsified or mixed.

Avocado Dip
Makes 1 1/2 cups

Ingredients

1 medium avocado, pitted and peeled
½ cup plain yogurt
¼ cup low fat sour cream
2 teaspoons fresh lime juice
2 Tablespoon minced onion
2 Tablespoons chopped fresh cilantro (if desired)
2 Tablespoons toasted chia seeds (see page 9)
Salt to taste

Directions

In a medium sized bowl, mash the avocado and lime juice until smooth. Stir in the remaining ingredients mixing until smooth. Add salt if using. Chill at least 30 minutes before serving.

SMOOTHIES / DRINKS

Fresca Chia Drink
One Serving

is one of the original ways that chia was used in the Aztec times and is even drink this way in the plaza's of Mexico City today.

For each serving add about 1 tablespoon of chia seeds to a large drinking glass. Add the juice of half of a lime (or to taste) or you can use lemon juice if you prefer. Add sugar or other sweetener to taste. Add cold water and stir until the sugar or sweetener is dissolved. You can add ice. Best drunk cold. You need to prepare ready before serving as the longer the chia is in the water the more "gel" like the beverage will become.

A refreshing treat for all ages anytime of the year.

A Shake, Rattle and Yum Drink
Makes 2 large glasses

Ingredients

2 chopped bananas
2 cups of your favorite milk - skimmed, rice, soy, nut
2 scoops of vanilla ice cream or ice milk or frozen yogurt
2 Tablespoons store brought caramel sauce
1 Tablespoon malted milk powder
2 Tablespoons chia seeds

Directions

Place all the ingredients into a blend and process until smooth. Pour and enjoy.

Early Morning Get Out the Door Drink
Makes 2 large glasses

Ingredients

2 chopped bananas
1 mango peeled, seeded and chopped
2 cups skim milk or soy milk, nut milk
2 cups orange juice
2 Tablespoons chia seeds

Directions
Place all the ingredients into a blend and process until smooth.
Pour and enjoy

Chia Lassi
Makes 2 large glasses

Ingredients

¼ cup lime juice
¼ cup sugar
¾ cup really good yogurt - the tangier the better
1 ½ cups coconut milk or any other kind of milk you prefer
9 to 10 ice cubes
2 Tablespoons chia seed

Directions

Place all the ingredients into a blender and process until smooth and creamy. Pour into glasses.

Chia Papaya Smoothie
Makes 2 large glasses

Ingredients

1 orange peeled and chopped
1 papaya seeded, peeled and chopped
8 to 9 ice cubes
1 cup plain yogurt
1 small peach peeled, seeded and chopped
2 Tablespoons honey
1 teaspoon vanilla extract
2 Tablespoons chia seed

Directions

Place all the ingredients into a blender and process until smooth and creamy. Pour into glasses.

Chia Avocado Smoothie
Makes 2 large glasses

Ingredients

1 Avocado, seeded, peeled and chopped
2 Cups your choice of milk - soy, cow's, rice or nut
1 Tablespoon honey
1 teaspoon vanilla extract
2 Tablespoons chia seed

Directions

Place all the ingredients into a blender and process until smooth and creamy. Pour into glasses.

Chia Cherry Smoothie
Makes 2 large glasses

Ingredients

2 cups almond milk
2 cups cherries, pitted
1 teaspoon vanilla extract
2 Tablespoons chia seed

Directions

Place all the ingredients into a blender and process until smooth and creamy. Pour into glasses.

Chia Aloha Smoothie
Makes 2 large glasses

Ingredients

2 Mangoes seeded, peeled and chopped
1 1/3 cups Milk - soy, cow's, rice or nut
1 cup pineapple juice
½ cup fresh mint leaves
8 ice cubes
2 Tablespoons chia seed

Directions

Place all the ingredients into a blender and process until smooth and creamy. Pour into glasses.

Chia Breakfast Smoothie
Makes 2 large glasses

Ingredients

2 cups Milk - soy, cow's, rice or nut
2 Bananas chopped
½ cup plain or vanilla yogurt
1 cup breakfast cereal
2 Tablespoons chia seed

Directions

Place all the ingredients into a blender and process until smooth and creamy. Pour into glasses.

Chia Tofu Smoothie
Makes 2 large glasses

Ingredients

2 cups Chocolate Milk - soy, cow's, rice or nut
2 Bananas chopped
2/3 cup silken tofu
2 Tablespoons honey
1 Tablespoon peanut butter
2 Tablespoons chia seed
8 to 10 ice cubes

Directions

Place all the ingredients into a blender and process until smooth and creamy. Pour into glasses.

Chia Fruit Slushy
Makes 2 large glasses

Ingredients

2 cups cranberry juice
2 ½ cups frozen raspberries
1 tablespoon honey or sugar
1 cup vanilla yogurt or plain yogurt with a teaspoon
    of vanilla extract
2 Tablespoons chia seed
8 to 10 ice cubes

Directions

Place all the ingredients into a blender and process until smooth and creamy. Pour into glasses.

Mint Julep with Chia without Bourbon
Serves 2

Ingredients

1 cup fresh mint leaves, chopped
1 Tablespoon sugar
½ Cup boiling water
1 Tablespoon lemon juice
1 Cup pineapple juice
1 Cup ginger ale
3 Tablespoons chia seed
Ice Cubes

Directions

In a heatproof pitcher place the mint leaves and sugar. Using the back of a wooden spoon lightly bruise the mint to release the oils. Add the lemon juice, pineapple juice and ½ cup boiling water, mix well. Cover and set aside for 30 minutes. Strain and then refrigerate at least 1 hour.

Just before serving, stir in the chia and ginger ale. Serve over ice.

Iced Peppermint Tea
Serves 2

Ingredients

2 Peppermint tea bags
3 ¼ cups boiling water
Zest of one lemon
1 Tablespoon sugar or to taste
4 Tablespoons chia seed
Ice cubes to serve

Directions

In a heatproof bowl or measuring cup put the tea bags, lemon zest and boiling water. Set aside to infuse for about 5 minutes. Squeeze out the tea bags and discard. Stir in the sugar. Chill for at least 1 hour. To serve, stir in the chia seeds, pour over ice and enjoy.

Strawberry Smoothie
Serves 2

Ingredients

1 ½ Cups strawberries, hulled
1 cup vanilla yogurt
2 cups Strawberry frozen yogurt
½ teaspoons vanilla extract
4 Tablespoons chia seed

Directions.

Place the strawberries, yogurt and vanilla in a blender. Blender until smooth. Add the chia seeds and pour into two tall glasses.

DESSERTS & OTHER GOOD STUFF

Nobby Apple Cake
Serves 8 large servings

Ingredients

1 Cup Sugar
2 Tablespoons shortening or butter
1 egg well beaten
3 cups apples, peeled, cored and seeded chopped in to small dice
¼ Cups walnuts or raisins
1 Teaspoon vanilla
1 Cup all-purpose flour
½ Teaspoons nutmeg freshly grated
¼ Teaspoon salt
½ Teaspoon baking powder
½ Teaspoon baking soda
½ cup milk
¼ cup chia seeds

Directions

Preheat oven to 350 degrees

Prepare a large round cake pan such as a 9" spring form with vegetable spray.

In a small bowl add the chia seeds to the milk and set aside.

In a large mixing bowl, cream the sugar and butter. Slowly add all other dry ingredients until mixed. Add the milk and chia mixture and mixed until smooth. Remove the bowl from the mixture, stir in the apples and either the nuts or raisins until combined. Pour the mixture into the prepared baking pan. Bake for 40 to 45 minutes. Cake will be lumpy -- nobby.

Serve hot or cold with or without the sauce .

Nobby Apple Cake Sauce

Ingredients

1 Cup sugar
¼ Teaspoon nutmeg freshly grated
2 Teaspoons all-purpose flour
Pinch of salt

2 Cups boiling water

Directions

In a saucepan over medium heat, boil 2 cups of water. Add the other ingredients and continue to boil for 5 minutes. Remove from the stove , add 1 Tablespoon lemon extract if desired. Pour over the cake or place in a bowl for individual servings.

Very Simple Fruit Dessert
Serves One

Ingredients

A mixture of your favorite fruit - sliced apples, sliced oranges, peeled and sliced banana, kiwi sliced, cherries, or any fruits of your choice.

2 Tablespoons of chia seed

4 ounces of fruit juice of your choice

Directions

Place the fruit in a cereal bowl, sprinkle with the chia seeds and pour the juice over the top. Stir until the seeds are in the juice. Let set about 10 minutes stirring to remove the lumps of seeds. After the 10 minutes, the chia and the juice will have formed into gel almost like a soft set gelatin type pudding surrounding the fruit with the gel.

Sure you can top this with whipped cream type topping if you desire.

A great treat for the kids or the kid in all of us.

Chia Cherry Berry Pie
Serves 8

Ingredients
1 can cherry pie filling
12 ounces of frozen mixed berries thawed and drained
¼ cup chia seeds
1 teaspoons vanilla extract
1 box ready made pie crust or your own recipe
Optional
1 egg lightly beaten
1 Tablespoon sugar

Directions

Preheat oven to 375 degrees.

In a large mixing bowl, combine the cherry pie filling, berries, chia seed and vanilla.

Place one of the pie crust in the bottom on a 9 inch pie pan. Pour the chia cherry pie filling into the crust. Gently fold the top crust over the filling. Crimp the edges, cut off the excess. Make a pattern in the top crust so that the steam can be released as the pie bakes.

Optional - Brush the top of the crust with the egg and sugar for a lightly browned look.

Bake 40 minutes. Remove from oven and let cool on a rack for at least 20 minutes before serving.

Old Fashion Fruit Cobbler
Serves 6

Ingredients
1 stick butter
1 cup flour
1 cup sugar
2 teaspoons Baking Powder
¾ cup milk
¼ cup chia seed
Pinch of salt
3 to 4 cups of fruit - berries, peaches, any family favorite fresh, frozen or canned drained.

Directions

Preheat oven to 350 degrees.

Melt the butter in the 9 inch square pan you are going to use to bake the cobbler.

In a mixing bowl combine the flour, baking powder, sugar, milk, chia seed, salt. When combined pour over the melted butter, topping with the fruit. Bake 45 minutes. Server if whipped cream or ice cream if desired. Can be served hot or room temperature.

Chia Fruit Leather sometimes called Fruit Rollups.

Apple Sauce works well in fruit leather but any fruit or berries will work.

Use chia gel (see page 9)

Mix ¼ chia gel to the fruit.

Puree the choice of mixed fruit or berries or single fruit or berries in a food processor or blender. Stir in the chia gel.

You can either dry the leather in a food dehydrator. Follow the directions that come with the dehydrator and use the leather trays.

Or you can oven dry by lining baking sheets with plastic wrap, smooth the fruit and chia mixture into a uniform layer. Place in a 140 degree oven overnight or longer until the leather is dry.

After the leather is dry, it can be cut into strips and rolled. Stored in a airtight container or wrapped in plastic wrap.

Date Nut Bread
Makes 1 loaf

Ingredients
1 cup brown sugar packed
1 Tablespoon melted butter
1 egg well beaten
¼ teaspoon salt
2 cups all-purpose flour
3 mashed ripe bananas
4 Tablespoon baking powder
1 Cup dates chopped
1 Cup boiling water
1 Teaspoon Vanilla
1 Cup Walnuts
1 Cup milk
4 Tablespoons chia seeds

Directions

Preheat oven to 350 degrees

Spray a loaf pan with vegetable spray

In a small heat proof bowl, pour the boiling water over the dates and chia seeds and let stand till cool.

Cream the butter and sugar until light and fluffy. Add the egg and date mixture and mix until combined. On low speed, add in the alt, baking soda and flour mix until combined. Mix until combined. Pour into the prepared loaf pan.

Bake for 1 hour or until a toothpick inserted in the middle comes out clean. Let cool on a wire rack for 15 minutes. Remove from the loaf pan.

Mama's Old Fashion Banana Bread
Makes 1 loaf

Ingredients

1 cup sugar
1 Tablespoon butter or shortening
1 egg
¼ teaspoon salt
1 ½ cup all-purpose flour
3 mashed ripe bananas
1 Teaspoon baking soda
1 Tablespoon water
4 Tablespoons chia seeds

Directions

Preheat oven to 300 degrees

Spray a loaf pan with vegetable spray

In a large mixing bowl, cream the butter or shortening with the sugar until light and fluffy. Add the egg and bananas and mix until combined. On low speed, add in the salt, baking soda and flour mix until combined. Add the water and chia. Mix until combined. Pour into the prepared loaf pan.

Bake for 1 hour or until a toothpick inserted in the middle comes out clean. Let cool on a wire rack for 15 minutes. Remove from the loaf pan.

Honey Roasted Nuts
Makes 8 cups

Ingredients

8 cups your choice of nuts - peanuts, almonds, cashews, walnuts it doesn't matter
1 ½ teaspoons salt
1 tablespoon water
2 tablespoons honey
2 tablespoons walnut or vegetable oil
½ cup chia seeds

Directions

Preheat oven to 375 degrees. Spread nuts out on a baking sheet with edges. Toast the nuts for 8 to 10 minutes.

While the nuts are roasting, in a very large skillet (preferred non-stick) over high heat combine the salt, water, honey, oil until the mixture is boiling. Immediately stir in the warm nuts and chia seed - stirring until all the glaze is stuck to the nuts and chia and the pan is dry. This will take just a couple of minutes.

Spray the baking sheet with cooking spray and return the nuts to the baking sheet in a single layer. Place them back in the oven for 2 minutes. Remove the sheet from the oven but leave the nuts on the sheet until cool. After the nuts are cooled, store in an airtight container.

Bread Machine Whole Wheat Bread

INGREDIENTS

1-1/2 cup plus 2 tablespoons water
2 tablespoons vegetable oil
2 teaspoons salt
1/3 cup packed brown sugar or honey
4-1/4 cups whole wheat flour
3 tablespoons nonfat dry milk
2 teaspoons active dry yeast
¼ cup chia seeds

Directions

Place ingredients in bread pan in order listed or according to manufacturer's directions. When adding the yeast last, make a small well with your finger to place the yeast. This will insure the proper timing of the yeast reaction.

Use Whole Wheat or Timed Cycle, or according to manufacturer's directions.

Chia Gluten Free White Bread
For both oven and bread machines
Makes 1 loaf

Ingredients

Yeast 2 teaspoons active dry yeast for a bread machine
Or 2 ½ teaspoons active dry yeast for the oven method
¼ cup chia seeds
1 Tablespoons potato flour
2 Tablespoons sugar or other sweetener of your choice
¾ teaspoon Lecithin Granules
1 teaspoon Guar Gum
1 ½ cups warm about 102 degrees milk of your choice - soy, nut, rice or cow's)
¾ cup whole egg or egg substitute
¼ Cooking oil - prefer vegetable type
1 teaspoon cider vinegar
½ teaspoon salt.

For bread machine:

In a large bowl mix all the dry ingredients until combined.

In another bowl add all the liquid ingredients and stir or whisk together until smooth.

Follow your bread machine's instructions for the order that ingredients are added. Set the controls for white bread and bake. Remove from the machine to cool.

For oven baking:

Proof the yeast in a small bowl by mixing the yeast to the warm milk - let set about 5 minutes.

While the yeast is proofing. In a large mixing bowl either by hand or a heavy duty stand mixer, combine all the ingredients and mix until just combined. Then add the yeast/milk mixture and mix until a soft ball is formed and all the ingredients have been combined.

Place the dough in a nonstick 9 x 5 inch greased loaf pan. Smooth the dough with a spatula. Cover with plastic wrap and let rise until the dough is level with the top of the pan. This will usually take about 40 minutes. Place the pan in a preheated 375 degree oven and bake for 60 to 65 minutes. When done, remove the bread from the pan and let cool on a wire rack

Chia, Oranges, Strawberries with Lime
Serves 4

Ingredients

8 ounces fresh strawberries, cleaned, hulled and sliced
3 oranges, peeled, sectioned with the membrane removed
½ cup chia seeds
2 Tablespoons sugar
1 lime juiced and the zest removed

Directions

Place all the ingredients in a large bowl, mix until combined, chill at least 30 minutes. Serve in a pretty bowl.

Frozen Peaches 'n Cream
Serves 4

Ingredients

1 ½ cups crushed vanilla wafers
¼ c melted butter
½ cup chia seeds
½ pound marshmallows
1 cup heavy cream whipped
2 Tablespoons orange juice
1 Tablespoon lemon juice
1 cup crushed peaches

Directions

Combine the vanilla wafer crumbs, butter and chia in a small bowl. Press into an 8" square pan covering the sides and bottom.

In a saucepan, combine the fruit juices and bring to a boil. Add the marshmallows and stir until dissolved. Remove from heat and cool. Add the peaches and stir until combined. Fold in the whipped cream. Pour into the prepared crust. Cover with plastic wrap or foil. Freeze 3 to 4 hours. Cut into squares and serve.

Ruth's Cookie Squares
Serves - well it depends on how well you like them

Ingredients

6 ounces chocolate chips
2 cups crushed graham crackers
½ cup chopped Marchino cherries
1 can sweetened condensed milk

Shredded coconut and/or chopped nuts if desired.

Directions

Preheat oven to 350 degrees

Prepare an 8" square baking pan with cooking spray.

In a mixing bowl add the chocolate chips graham cracker crumbs, Marchino cherries and condensed milk, stir until combined. Pour into the prepared pan. Smooth the top of the mixture and if desired sprinkle with the coconut and nuts.

Bake 35 minutes.

Remove from the oven, cool on a wire rack. To serve, cut into squares.

Old Fashioned Blueberry Pudding
Serves 10 to 12

Ingredients
3 Cups Blueberries
1 Cup packed brown sugar
6 Tablespoons butter
1 Cup sugar
2/3 Cup butter at room temp.
½ Teaspoon vanilla
1 ½ cups all-purpose flour
2 Teaspoons baking powder
½ Teaspoon salt
2 Teaspoons orange zest
¾ Cup orange juice
½ Cup chia seeds
2 Eggs
Whipped Cream for topping or ice cream as desired.

Directions

Preheat oven to 350 degrees.

Over medium heat in a sauce pan, simmer blueberries, brown sugar and 6 tablespoons of butter for about 10 minutes. With a mixer cream together the sugar, 2/3 cup butter and vanilla. Add the eggs and mix until combined. Sift the flour, baking powder and salt into the sugar/butter mixture. Add the orange juice and zest and chia seeds. Put the blueberry mixture in the bottom of a 3 quart baking dish. Pour the batter over the berries. Bake 45 minutes. Serve at room temperature topped with whipped cream or ice cream.

Raspberry Kuchen
Makes 16 Squares

Ingredients

1 egg well beaten
½ Cup milk
1 Cup all-purpose flour
1 Cup fresh or thawed frozen raspberries
½ Cup sugar
2 Tablespoons vegetable oil
2 Teaspoons baking power
½ Cup chia seeds

Topping
½ Cup all-purpose flour
3 Tablespoons cold butter
½ Cup sugar

Directions

Preheat oven to 375 degrees.

In a bowl, combine egg, sugar, milk and oil, mixing well. Sift together the flour and baking powder, stir into the egg mixture. Add the chia seed and mix until combined. Pour into a vegetable sprayed 8 inch square pan. Sprinkle raspberries over the batter. For the topping: in a small box, mix the flour and sugar, cut in the butter until the mixture resembles coarse crumbs. Sprinkle topping over raspberries. Bake 25 to 30 minutes until a toothpick stick in the center comes out clean. Best served warm.

Printed in the United States
110714LV00006B/49/A